FOR AND AFTER

For and After CHRISTOPHER REID

faber and faber

First published in 2003
by Faber and Faber Limited
3 Queen Square London WC1N 3AU
Published in the United States by Faber and Faber Inc.
an affiliate of Farrar, Straus and Giroux LLC, New York

Typeset by Faber and Faber Limited
Printed in England by T J International Ltd, Padstow, Cornwall

A CIP record for this book
is available from the British Library
ISBN 0-571-21807-5

10 9 8 7 6 5 4 3 2 1

Contents

For and After
for Lucinda

While

for Lucinda

While you were confined to the gloom
of our hushed and shuttered room,
I stepped out into the sun.
Olive-trees all the way down
to the hidden, then sudden valley,
where I hoped to see things more clearly:
each tree with unique, twisted grace
asserting rights in that harsh place,
hugging its shade to itself
while flaunting an enigmatic wealth
of drab, yet glittering foliage,
under which – and this was the knowledge
I'd come for – it formed its fruit
from a pressure like unspoken thought.

Palace Floor

for Seamus Heaney

The calculations and accidents of the kiln
that gave such depth and difference to the tesserae,
their earth and flesh tones, unanalysably tertiary,
by which the breasts and pot-belly of the Sea Goddess
were made so round and real that he was scared to caress them,
drew him again and again to inspect that chamber,
and even when forced abroad he would seem to hear her,
from her company of octopus and swordfish, calling, calling.

Broken Journey

for Chiara, Elena and Alba, at the Fattoria Mosè

Like an inexpert angler
      on the bank of a river
in which he knows
      there must be fish
and fish in great number
      though not to be caught by him
I sat at your table
      and listened entranced
to the superabundance
      the quirky currents
the dazzle and dash
      of your conversation and laughter

A time of sickness
      a time of anxiety
yet I seemed to have wandered
      into a land of plenty
where not just your spirited
      hospitality
the family table cluttered
      with dishes and glasses
but a sense too
      of unhindered possibility
was given voice
      even as the details escaped me

On Upland Pastures
after Satta

So, that bright shaft was just
a brief dream of the sun,
and the long, cold, lasting
shadows settle down

across the wild highlands.
The grieving earth now reaches
in its starkness and silence
as far as the distant peaks.

A solitary shepherd
with cloak and bundle stands
watching this dark, ice-hard
and storm-prone land.

To Sylvia

after Leopardi

Sylvia, do you remember
that day of all your days
when your shy glance kindled
to a ravishing blaze,
and at once thoughtful and cheerful
you set your foot
on the threshold of young womanhood?

Your non-stop singing
carried indoors and out,
as you went sedately about
your girlish tasks,
perfectly content
with the bland and hazy future
you assumed life was bringing.
It was a fragrant May –
and that's how you spent your day.

Forgetting for once
the studies that so enthralled me –
those scribbled pages
at which I sweated for ages,
wasting the best of my life –
I would lean from the balcony
outside my father's room,
straining to catch your voice
and the faint racket you made
as you busied yourself at your loom.
I was dazzled by
the untroubled sky,

the sun-gilt streets and the gardens.
No mortal tongue can tell
what I felt then.

Darling Sylvia,
what delicious things we imagined,
what hopes and longings we had!
And how splendid it must have seemed –
the human condition!
When I think now of all we dreamed,
disgust and despair
come down hard
and I'm sent back to grieve
over everything gone wrong.
O Nature, Nature,
why do you never deliver
what you once promised?
Why must you always deceive
the children who trust you?

Even before winter
had shrivelled the leaves,
ambushed and overpowered
by some rogue disease,
you died, poor little one.
And so you never saw
your life in full flower;
never felt the pleasure
of being flattered
on your wonderful black hair,
or your smitten and bashful eyes;
never chattered
about love and such things
on jolly holiday outings.

My future, too, died
soon after that;
I, too, was denied
the fulfilment of youth.
How completely you have vanished,
dear companion of those early years,
my hope, now greatly lamented.
Can this be the world we wanted?
These, the delights, the passions,
the adventures and the glories
about which we told such stories?
This, the human lot?
At the first hint of the truth,
you fell, unlucky girl,
with a gesture indicating
death and an unadorned tomb
in the distance, waiting.

Last Flowers

after Pushkin

The season's last flowers yield
more than those first in the field.
The thoughts they rouse – sharp, sweet –
have an incomparable power;
likewise, the parting hour
as against when we merely meet.

French Kisses

The Ladybird
after Hugo

'Something's itching,' she said,
and there, the one speck
on her flawless neck,
was a ladybird, shockingly red.

I ought . . . I ought to have seen,
not that bug ambulating,
but the kiss she had waiting –
but aren't we all shy at sixteen?

It was like a rare shell, with black
spots on its scarlet back.
Every neighbouring rook
leant out of its nest for a closer look.

Her lips were right there;
I leant, too, and captured
that ladybird,
while the kiss flew off into thin air.

Then the insect addressed me from heaven:
'Young man, take this as a sign
that the so-called brutes are divine,
only brute stupidity human.'

The Ghost of the Rose
  after Gautier

Come, blinking, out of a doze
dream-fevered and virginal . . .
I am the ghost of a rose
you wore at yesterday's ball.
You picked me with spangles of dew
from the sprinkler still heavy on me,
and displayed me all evening through
to that glittering company.

Because of you, I am dead.
Now nothing you do will keep
me from dancing each night at the head
of your bed, as you try to sleep.
But be brave: let no bell toll,
no requiem mass be heard;
this waft of perfume is my soul,
and Paradise my reward.

There's many a man would have given
everything he possessed
to achieve an equivalent heaven,
my tomb being your breast.
And to mark my repose,
some poet or other wrote this:
'Here lies the most envied rose
in the world' – then added a kiss.

Romance without Words
  after Verlaine

The piano, which someone's delicate hand is kissing,
gleams indistinctly through the blush and gloom
of dusk, and all the while, with wingbeats barely assisting,

a song, as compelling as it is old and faint,
sweeps cautiously, fearfully even, through the room
that has for so long borne traces of her scent.

What is this lullaby which all of a sudden
is gently rocking and soothing my wretched soul?
What do you want from me, sweet, teasing air?

What *was* it you wanted, hovering and dithering here,
before passing with a dying fall
through a window just open on to the little garden?

The Sirens

after Homer and for Christopher Logue

As I was putting my men in the picture,
a fair wind brought us abreast
of the Sirens' island, then dropped.
Dead calm. Waves spellbound.
But the crew leapt straight up, furled the sail
and stowed it, then back at their oars
whipped the water till it blazed white.
I took a slab of wax, chopped it,
kneaded it, and soon, with the sun's help,
it was soft enough to stop the ears
of my shipmates. And they in turn
stood me against the mast and lashed me
tightly to it. Then back to their oars again.
Just as we came within hailing distance,
the Sirens, catching sight of our progress,
sent out this eerily voluptuous song:

> *Draw near, Odysseus, pride of the Achaians,*
> *lay to awhile and listen to our voices.*
> *No one has ever yet sailed past this island*
> *without hearing the music of our sweet lips*
> *or going on his way a wiser man.*
> *We know what was suffered on the plains of Troy*
> *by Argives and Trojans, at the whim of the gods.*
> *We know all that happens on this bountiful earth.*

That's what they sang. I wanted to hear more,
so I yelled at my shipmates and shook my frenzied head at
    them,
but they leant to their oars and pulled and pulled,
while Perimedes and Eurylochos

jumped up, found some extra rope
and tied me even tighter.
Once we'd left the Sirens behind us
and were out of range of their outlandish voices,
my men removed the wax from their ears
and freed me from my own confinement.

Five Fires

after Philodemos

Serena's accomplishments,
her dancing, her smart chatter,
her voluble eyes, her electric voice,
and the fire they are busy kindling
      will burn you through and through, my heart –
precisely when and where
and in what particular manner,
I can't say yet, but you'll know,
unhappy giblet,
      just as soon as you start sizzling.

    *

One last kerfuffle
      of coals in the grate,
old eavesdropper
      on our most burning secrets –
and that will be all, Phelps.
      Good night. And shut the door, will you?
I believe we can manage
      without a spectator.

Now, Cynthia darling,
      it's getting late . . .

Stand by, bedsprings!
      I hope you're ready
for your next practical lesson
      in the Kama Sutra.

    *

Night-prowling crescent moon,
        always looking out for fun,
take a peek through this window
        at my honey-bundle Corinna.

As a heavenly celebrity,
        of course you're allowed to snoop;
and we're touched by your interest, moon.
        Why, wasn't it Endymion
who once set your soul on fire?

        *

Light?
        Cheers.
And you're?
        You first.
Nosy.
        Who's talking?
Alone?
        Depends.
Hungry?
        You said it.
I suppose . . .
        Not here.
Really?
        Later.
Where, then?
        That way.
Now?
        Up to you.
Ah . . .
        Come on.

        *

Summer's flowers
        are still tight in their buds,
and her grapes yet to round out
        and deepen their colour,
but already the baby bowmen
are preparing their arrows
        and the very air seems combustible.

Let's get out of here, Kimberly –
        we've neither of us been lucky in love.
Quick now: they're taking aim
and a twinge in my big toe tells me
        major conflagration!

Age

after Ronsard

The future; faltering firelight;
and funny . . . who's that I see
mumbling the poetry
yours truly used to write?

What a rotten shame:
no one at hand to hear –
let alone pretend to care –
that that was *your* undying name.

Bones tucked away, my ghost
will be up with the heavenly host,
while you clatter the grate

of your pride and your sorrow . . .
Now come on, forget tomorrow,
which was always too late.

Bag

after Hadrian

A plastic bag
the wind must have snatched and lifted
that must have drifted
bellying like a sail
one minute
      limp
      crumpled and plunging
the next
      then –
            puny featureless unclaimed soul –
buoyant again
but always
subject to the jitters
of cross-currents and thermals
until it met the snag
      of the pavement sycamore's outstretched branch
now hangs exposed
to all winter weathers –
            where next being scarcely an issue –
like a dirty flag.

Song of the Godparents

for Alex Zagórska-Thomas

Hello, little pip.
How do you do, little squiggle –
with your unsteady stare
and your finger grip
that is lighter than air
and your vigorous wriggle.
We hope you enjoyed your trip.

Welcome to our world,
little dot, little notion,
and good luck as you start
to make sense of the huge commotion
at the very heart
of which you are quizzically curled,
of which you are the newest part.

Though we cannot tell
your fortune, little inkling,
loved as you are
we think you should both do well
and journey far.
So be brave, little twinkling,
tentative but wishable star.

Flies

after Machado

Dear common flies,
  ubiquitous and greedy,
    how well you conjure up
      those times that have gone.
Old flies guzzling
  like bees in April,
    old flies launching raids
      on my new-born head.
Flies of my early
  home-bound boredoms,
    those summer afternoons
      when I first learnt to dream.
And in the hated classroom,
  flies that whizzed past
    as we hit out at them
      for love of their flight –
flying being everything –
  and that buzzed against the windowpanes
    on autumn days . . .
      Flies for all seasons:
for infancy and puberty,
  for my gilded youth,
    for this, my second childhood
      of innocence and unbelief,
for now and forever . . . Common flies,
  you're too promiscuous
    to have found an adequate singer:
      I know how you've dallied

on marvellous toys,
      on the covers of books,
            on love letters,
                  on the unblinking eyelids
of corpses.
      Ubiquitous and greedy,
            lazier than bees
                  and scruffier than butterflies,
piffling, unruly,
      you're old friends, nonetheless,
            as you conjure up
                  those times that have gone.

Smoking, Drinking, etc.

A Pipe
after Baudelaire

I am a poet's pipe.
Cursory inspection
of my African complexion
will tell you he's the hard-smoking type.

When things are really bad,
I send up puffs as steady
as from some cottage where supper's ready
for the homecoming farm lad.

To keep his soul calm,
I can make a swaying hammock unroll
in blue wisps from my fiery bowl

and spread a potent balm,
soothing to his heart and kind
to his exhausted mind.

At the Green Man
  after Rimbaud

For a week now, I'd been blistering my feet
on the stony country roads. Then I came to Hemel Hempstead.
At the Green Man, I asked for some French bread,
butter, and ham with still a hint of its oven heat.

Contentedly stretching my legs under the green-topped table,
I'm studying the décor, when – wa-hey! up flies
the bar-girl with her voluminous tits and flashing eyes.
(Getting past those defences shouldn't prove much trouble.)

She smiles as she hands me a big Staffordshire dish
of bread already buttered and home-baked ham,
all pink and white and keen to hail everyone
with garlicky bonhomie. Plus, there's a bottle to replenish
my long glass, which instantly heaves up oodles of foam
in its haste to be blessed by a last-minute ray of the sun.

Cigar Smoke
  after Mallarmé

The whole soul summed up
as we breathe it out
in a few leisurely puffs
that dissolve in the general cloud

attests to a cigar
burning capably
so long as its bright fire
kisses the ash goodbye

likewise should your lips
give wing to some sentimental song
be sure to omit
anything real or debasing

too clear a sense destroys
literature's mysteries.

Genoa
  after Valéry

Perfumed paths
where one breathes
such abundance, such a hubbub
of narcotic spells,

yet where, prowling nose,
you snub
all smells
from the muddled shadows . . .

You know the lie
of the land?
        – Yes, and I don't need help
from *your* bleary eye.

No sense defying
the come-and-get-me yelp
of something frying.

Memoirs of a Publisher
after Li Po

Such a good lunch
suddenly it's evening

crumbs on the tablecloth
I totter outside

where have the pigeons gone?
where are the taxis?

Ant and Grasshopper

after La Fontaine

The grasshopper sang his song
all summer long,
then found himself skint
at the first hint of winter –
not even a bit of fly or grub-meat
to put on his plate.
Faint with hunger, he went
to his neighbour, the ant,
begging him for some grain
to sustain him through the lean season.
'I'll pay you back by August the first,'
he promised, 'with interest.
On my honour!' The ant was never,
sadly, the most open-handed of hymenoptera.
'What were you doing when the weather was warm?'
he wanted the beggar to tell him.
'Singing, night and day, to whoever happened along.
Anything wrong?'
'Singing?' was the ant's reply. 'Well, fancy that!
Now's your chance to dance.'

Olympiad

after Aesop

Six creatures ran:
a pig, a duck, a man,
a rabbit and a tortoise –
number six, a flea,
being impossible to see.

According to reporters,
the man passed the post
hours ahead of the rest,
which was hardly the greatest sport, as
I think you'll agree –

though surprising sums were lost
in flutters on the tortoise,
and one eccentric spectator
many years later
was still contending the flea
had been robbed of the cup,
till at last they locked him up.

There Was a Tree
for Monika Beisner

There was a tree that did not fly and did not speak.
   No pouting princess was imprisoned in its trunk.
It never cuddled the full moon in its branches. No Greek
   nymph's death was figured there forever. No pen-pushing monk
conceived canticles to it as to the Holy Cross.
   Its timber never furnished a boat that could not be sunk.
Dragons came nowhere near it, evidently. Plain moss,
   and nothing to do with sumptuous fabric, spread to one side.
It bore fruit, and not babies. Its bark was a total loss,
   so far as the countering of curses was concerned. No one died
from sleeping in its shade. Its tip fell far short of a hundred
   miles, and it was less than ten days' gallop wide.
No blood, just sap, ran through it. Thieves would have plundered
   its blossom in vain. Ghosts, jewelled snakes, mad kings
and riddling crows were foreign to it. Had you wandered
   past it at midnight, you would never have heard devils' wings.
Nor would its leaves have heard you. Its root,
   plunged fervently into the stony heart of things,
would not have allowed it to follow you home. The root was not
     a foot.
   And the tree was not a fire. Unblazing, it would have stayed put.

A City that Marco Polo Missed
for Sara Fanelli

Whatever the nature of your journey, whether you've been
    tossed
this way and that on the blustery epic of the Atlantic Ocean,
thwarted by the tangled syntax of the Brazilian jungle, or lost
somewhere in the interminable theological treatise of the
    Sahara,
there is no more pleasant emotion
than to find yourself suddenly at the gates of the city of Sara.

Because it is always on the move, its precise extent is a
    mystery;
but the traveller who takes it in slowly, as it were a page at a
    time,
will learn something of its peculiar customs and history
and soon feel at home. Street manners are elaborately good;
there are skyscrapers, but no crime;
both birds and insects wear hats; the entire populace loves
    picnic food.

Arrows, asterisks and exclamation-marks are a major feature
of the local dialect, and musical notation hangs like fruit in
    the air.
You may occasionally run into some extravagant creature
with an odd number of legs, a whirligig tail or unmatching
    eyes,
but there is nothing to fear
in this perfectly egalitarian state, no one to dislike or despise.

People say that the architect and the law-giver of the city
were one and the same. Indeed, some believe it was a child,
who took a sheet of grown-up graph-paper and filled it with
    witty
frisks and twiddles, which then sprang to a life of their own.
This is a place that encourages wild
flights of fancy, but where no dog is without its necessary
    bone.

Bermudapest

for Clarissa Upchurch and George Szirtes

A place I've never been,
but which, at the back
of my mind's eye,
I know I've seen:

its stately apartment blocks
beginning to melt
in the mid-morning blaze,
its beach cafés

loud with the laughter
of chess-players and philosophers.
And there's the postcard view –
you'll know it –

down an avenue
of lolling palms,
where the Imperial Cavalry
once wheeled and stamped and jangled

under the indolent
scrutiny of a poet,
who, turning to his guitar,
strummed the first bar

of his improbable epic:
the high tones of history
flavoured
with a peppery patois,

a nonchalant beat added
to old Gypsy sorrows.
A good place to meet,
I feel, and clink

a glass or two
of something sombre as ink,
with a paper parasol in it.
Let's get on a plane and go there.

Tomorrow's?

Nine Triangles
for Breon O'Casey

Eyelight thrown
on a dark question
to darken it further.

Time to take in
the view, the entire
daily tablescape.

Earthenmost shades –
and yet the effect
is of airy redemption.

That pledge of mud
the soul needs
to make its abstract journey.

Shapes huddled
in improvised families
out of the storm of seeing.

Wedges, half-moons,
rough squares: a simple
bag of tricks.

But everything
is accounted for
by these economics.

The epicurean
saint attends
to his plot of paint.

The world beyond
staying just the same,
only more so.

Thirty-three Paroxysms
for Kay Henderson, in memory of Ewen

He talked like a pessimist and acted like an optimist.

His despair of humanity was one of humanity's best reasons for hope.

He spoke eloquently against the danger of words.

His hand gestures showed that for him ideas were tactile.

His jokes were profoundly silly.

Puns, spoonerisms and other verbal games were among his preferred oracular devices.

He had a nose for the essential – a broken nose.

He entrusted his weightiest statements to a fragile medium.

In his art, the creative and the destructive possibilities of fire were one and the same thing.

His pots were built as monuments to impermanence.

They have the repose of volcanoes.

They aspire to the condition of questions, not answers.

Most of his vessels leak.

Whether his bowls and dishes contain fruit or stand empty, they suggest cornucopias.

While his paintings explore three dimensions, his sculptural work meditates on four.

He pursued a vision of wholeness by means of collage.

His drawings do not confuse grace with gracefulness.

Prettiness, elegance, refinement and symmetry were all traps he took care to avoid.

His garden used a time-honoured English decorative art form to express new and outlandish truths.

Birds, frogs, slugs and insects know his work better than many art experts.

He despised most critics for betraying their art.

Music was his ideal form of sculpture.

Machaut, Gesualdo, Bach, Berlioz, Stravinsky and Ligeti were all his exact contemporaries.

He was a Modernist, of the school of Lascaux.

He believed in the eternal youth of the ancient world.

Nature was his culture.

Like any great teacher, he wanted us to teach ourselves.

His cat and his dog were his most attentive students, and he was theirs.

His anger sprang from generosity.

He was a gentle man whom the powerful found fierce.

He had great appetites but little greed.

Because he loved life, he accepted death.

Now that he is gone, we look for him everywhere.

A Scarecrow's Theory of Art
for Rob Woolner

Two eyes, peeled,
step into a field
of coloured mud.
The field is a flood
of marks and matter.
The field is a scatter
of planes and lines,
a system of signs
bounded by what
the field is not.
The field is a figment
of mind and pigment,
of hand and weather
working together
in conflict and discourse.
The field is a force.
The field is a field
where two eyes, peeled
to appraise the new
and eternal view
that the painter has made
from shape and shade,
feel the light
stiffen and bite
like a brisk gust
from nowhere, then must
begin gleaning
their own meaning.

The Crack
for Helen Wilks

A scary-precipitous game:
the child who should be asleep
has slithered from bed to peep
at the gap between door and frame –
a narrow, inscrutable flame.
Her dark eyes, fixed on it, keep
a distance we cannot leap,
but must try to all the same.

And isn't that your fix, too,
the Helen your paints recall,
with her hair in a grip and her blue
dressing-gown, clutching her small
chimp friend, being you and yet not you,
and yet possibly you after all?

Espionage

for Philomena Muinzer

It looks all flim-flam and fangles –
      wily schoolboy wangles,
passwords from *Alice in Wonderland*
      and code as a spiffing game.

But suppose that document there
      bore your stunned photo
and a stranger's name;
      now put it in the hands
      of some paper-chewer in uniform:
          the vertiginous moment expands . . .

And that is where you must live
as human camouflage,
      a life-shaped stage-flat dropped
      into a breathing landscape,
      sitting tight,
      sustained by a parsimonious
          drip of radio signals,
      waiting for something important
          to fall out of the night.

Doing the exhibition –
      you with your notebook, me with mine –
indulging *what if* and *perhaps*,
      I should like to own and then give you
      one of those maps
      of enemy territory
      printed on silk so fine
          they fold away almost to nothing:
      simple, accurate, secret,
          an unbeatable design.

Dogs and Ghosts
for Molly Sackler

Over tea at the Algonquin,
    where, among the witty ghosts,
that of Thurber, who loved to draw dogs –
    themselves like the ghosts of dogs –
haunts the mid-afternoon shadows
    more livingly than most,
you asked me about my own
    dog-populated poems.
Why so many? I couldn't
    explain it then, but lately
bumping into a dog I know,
    who, to judge by her torpedo greeting,
seemed to know me too,
    I saw what might be a clue
in the oddity, the imbalance,
    the *off*-balance of our meeting.
With their intemperate dashes at the barrier
    that's fixed between the species,
their sharp offal-huff and slaver
    aimed towards our faces,
their paws scrabbling at our chests
    in high-minded yearning to be
of us, and not just with us,
    dogs now strike me
as champion four-legged metaphors
    for metaphors: their use,
in a certain kind of poem,
    to be true to a parallel destiny
at much the same distance as ghosts are,
    only yappy and footloose.

Another of Daddy's Cats
for Ted Hughes

I was up, before the servants,
in Daddy's den.

The room had bottled and chilled
the heart-sinking smell
of last night's Dutch cheroots.

Snooker trophies,
a soda siphon that sneezed
at the lightest of touches

and that tiger forever
ramming its head through the wall:

all animated whiskers,
whisky-tinctured teeth
and popping, pale-ale eyeballs.

Rose Window
after Rilke

Inside, the *pad, pad* of paws
puts you in a daze;
and the way one of the cats secures
your wavering gaze

before absorbing it into its own deep eye –
your gaze, as if spun
on the dish of a whirlpool, somehow keeping dry
until sucked to oblivion

when the eye, calm as it may first have seemed,
opens and, with a roar, slams shut,
hauling it into the bloodstream –

that's how, awed
by a great cathedral window, the heart
used to be snatched from darkness and shot towards God.

Sahara

after Tsvetayeva

Young men, stop right where you are!
Wastes of sand now smother
and silence
your missing brother.

I'll tell you straight,
young men: the one you're looking for
is buried.
You've come too late.

Poetry,
as if through some country
of miracles and fire –
poetry first brought him to me:

parched, barren,
measureless, timeless.
Through some such country,
to my heart.

Listen to our story
and don't be jealous
that each in the other's eye
found an oasis.

Touched by the trembling of his Adam's apple,
I seized him
like a fit,
like God.

No name, no trace . . .
And the desert was always
a forgetful place,
so many sleep there.

Waves pound
and seethe and slither out flat;
and you, too, must let
me settle as your burial-mound.

The Phone-Fox

for Jane Feaver

We were talking about Ted Hughes,
    when the corner of my eye
twitched to the fact of a fox
    on the flat, tar-papered roof
of the chapel-of-rest next door.
    What a moment to choose!
I watched as it spelt itself out
    from shadows of the far-side garden
into clear sunlight,
    at which point I gave a shout
which must have sounded crazy.
    Then it trotted about,
inspecting different views.
    And then it did a quick jig
once around itself,
    lay down, extended its forepaws
and cocked its muzzle for a big,
    tasty, air-licking yawn.
Unbiddable, unbidden,
    this was a genuine fox
of the Inner London variety,
    now enjoying its own society
on top of the squat brick box
    where they bring the newly dead.
Accident or sign,
    I was sorry nothing I said
could make it real for you
    at your end of the line.

The Pickupine
for Katherine Pierpoint

The pickupine
(from Mexico)
puts on a fine
and furious show.

With quills banded
red, white and blue,
he might be a bandit
out to get *you*.

But look at his eyes,
so melancholy,
so mild, so wise,
and you'll see he's really

a misunderstood
and gentle beast,
not rough or rude –
no, not in the least.

While the porcupine
will stab and sting you,
the pickupine
simply wants to bring you

a handy set
of those sharp little sticks
that you sometimes get
labelled 'toothpicks'

or else are supplied
at cocktail parties
for piercing the hide
of chipolatas.

A sweet disposition
is the key feature
of this paradoxically bristling
Mexican creature.

Bollockshire

You've zoomed through it often enough
on the long grind north, the grim dash south –
        why not take a break?
        Slip off the motorway
at any one of ten tangled junctions
and poke your nose, without compunction,
        into the unknown.
        Get systematically lost.
At the first absence of a signpost,
opt for the least promising lane,
        or cut into the truck traffic
        along some plain,
perimeter-fence-lined stretch of blacktop
heading nowhere obvious.
        Open your mind
        to the jarring yellow
of that hillside rape crop, the grim Norse green
of that fir plantation, where every tree
        steps forward to greet you
        with the same zombie gesture
of exclamation, the last-ditch brown of –
what could it be? Something to do with pigs?
        Row on row
        of miniature Nissen huts
laid out like a new speculative estate
in acres of glistening mud, behind an electronic gate . . .
        But don't stop now.
        Press on,
undistracted by the lush hedgerows

(of which there are none)
        or the silence of the songbirds.
        Other counties
can match these. It's the essence of Bollockshire
you're after: its secrets, its blessings and bounties.
        So keep driving,
        past sly-windowed farms,
lying there with hoards of costly machinery
in their arms, like toys they won't share;
        past Bald Oak Hill,
        down the more shaded side of which
the Bollockshire Hunt has scuffled
many a morning to its kill;
        past St Boldric's church,
        with the slant steeple,
which Cromwell's lads once briefly visited,
leaving behind them saints re-martyred,
        the Virgin without her head;
        past Bewlake Manor's
dinky Gothic gatehouse, now the weekend habitat
of London media or money people;
        past the isolated
        Bulldog pub,
with its choice of scrumpies, microwave grub,
bouncy castle and back-room badger fights –
        past all that,
        until, if you are lucky,
you hit the famous ring road. Thrown down
decades ago, like a gigantic concrete garland
        around the county town,
        riddled and plugged
by the random dentistry of maintenance work
and chock-a-block with contraflow,

it must, you feel,
            be visible from the moon.
One road sign hides another. There are orange cones
galore. Each cultivated roundabout island
            is, if possible, more off-key
            than the one before.
But don't stick here all afternoon:
Blokeston itself has to be seen,
            via the brick maze
            of its bygone industrial outskirts.
This is where Silas Balk invented his machine
for putting a true, tight twist in string,
            where they once supplied the world
            with all it needed
of bicycle saddles and cigarette papers,
where cough syrup was king.
            Round the corner,
            just when you least expect,
there's Blokeston FC, home of 'The Blockers',
and Blokeston Prison, by the same no-frills architect.
            Unmissable from any position,
            the Bulwark Brewery
stands up in a haze of its own malty vapours,
which even today's counterwafts of tandoori
            cannot contest.
            Now, turn east or west,
and you'll find yourself on a traffic-planner's
one-way inward spiral, passing at speed
            through older and older
            parts of town –
the impeccable Georgian manners
of Beauclerc Square, built on slave-trade money;
            bad Bishop Bloggs's school;

the crossroads where
the Billhook Martyrs were tortured and burned –
until you reach the river Bleak.
            Squeeze, if you can,
            over the Black Bridge,
then park and pay – assuming this isn't the week
of the Billycock Fair, or Boiled Egg Day,
            when they elect the Town Fool.
            From here, it's a short step
to the Bailiwick Hall Museum and Arts Centre.
As you enter, ignore the display
            of tankards and manacles, the pickled head
            of England's Wisest Woman;
ask, instead, for the Bloke Stone.
Surprisingly small, round, featureless,
            pumice-grey,
            there it sits, dimly lit,
behind toughened glass, in a room of its own.
Be sure to see it, if you've a taste
            for this sort of primitive conundrum.
            Most visitors pass
and won't even leave their vehicles,
keen by this time to make haste
            back to the life they know,
            and to put more motorway under them.

Bush to Blair

You can't unthink the unthinkable,
>   and now is no longer the time to think.
Be like a rock, unsinkable,
>   as we take our respective positions over the brink
and into a new future.
>   Is this war? you ask.
Never mind the nomencluture;
>   we have a mighty historical task
on both our plate, plus a side order
>   of saving the world from total evil, or worse.
I say, let the marauder
>   be marauded back! Let a curse
be on his house,
>   even if he happens to live
in a hole in a rock, like the cowardly louse
>   he no question is. Lest we forgive –
heck, isn't that one of your own Saint Winston's
>   inspirational quotes? –
we must never forget for an instance
>   that it was the enemy burned our boats
for us and there can be no compromise.
>   Remember the old Crusades:
those movies with the crazy guys
>   with the swords with the non-straight blades
that could cut a lady's silk bandanna in half?
>   Sure, that was a neat trick,
but who had the last laugh?
>   I hope Bin Laden saw one one time and feels real sick!

Tom Cove

So that was your name –
as I learned from the bunches of flowers
still in their presentation cellophane,
placed at the end of the mews
by the spot where you collapsed.

Where you'd weathered many a raw day
swigging and foul-mouthing,
if not across in York Way
doing your tormented pavement dance
of shuffling and bowing and fleering.

Your free hand flung out big stagy gestures.
I caught little you said,
though in a thunderstorm one night –
'Turn off the lights!' you ranted back at Him.
'Go on, turn off the lights!'

Who didn't wish to be rid of you?
Yet here are these flowers and kind words
from local residents and shopkeepers,
offered up to your ghost
to explain how you'll be missed.

The Ruin
after the anonymous Anglo-Saxon

What a wall –
        though history's rubbished it,
smashed the buildings,
        swept the legendary
structures away.
        Roofs have collapsed,
towers tumbled,
        gates gape
and frost chews
        in between the stones.
Ceilings are useless:
        it was age did for them,
caved in,
        crashed to the ground.
Now earth holds
        in its unloving embrace
the great men
        who built these things.
Obliterated.
        Cancelled forever.
And generations
        have filed past
this same wall,
        ruddy-complexioned,
grizzled with lichen,
        and biding its time
while dynasties came and went
        and the weather

did its damnedest.
          Then the wall itself fell.
  [. . .]

It was a bold
          and ingenious conception:
the foundations
          could be made stronger
by a new system
          of metal girders
and linking bands.
          They built on the grandest scale,
bathhouses everywhere,
          cornices scraping the sky.
Oh, the noise of the place!
          The bars and the night life
palpitated –
          till events took a turn
and put a stop
          to all frivolity.
Mass slaughter
          was capped by pestilence.
Death picked off
          every last soul.
The fortifications
          stood deserted.
The city centre
          became wasteland.
Both warriors and builders
          lay for eternity
beyond recruitment.
          Which is why these buildings
fell as they did,
          their roof beams buckled

and they shrugged off their tiles.
                    Ruins seek flatness,
and yet mounds of rubble
                    can still be found,
to mark where men
                    in their pride and finery,
robust and wine-flushed,
                    once totted up
treasure beyond belief,
                    gold, silver
and precious gems;
                    or cast an eye
across the city
                    and its environs.

  [. . .]

The Snail
after Giusti

Here's to the snail
  here's to a beast
hopes for the best
  happy with the least
gave astronomers
  and architects
ideas for gadgets
  as complex
as telescope
  and spiral stair
here's to a creature
  we should all hold dear

Content with whatever's
  given by God
Diogenes
  the Gastropod
never ventures
  beyond his roof
settled in habits
  therefore proof
against such ills
  as the common cold
here's to the emblem
  of a good household

Fancy cuisines
  are designed to excite
the gourmet's pigged-out
  appetite

snail is always
        in perfect trim
home-grown dishes
        nourish him
new green shoots
        his favourite feast
here's to the frugal
        little beast

How to get by
        in a world without love
everyone a hawk
        no one a dove
look how snail
        avoids a spat
pulls in both horns
        just like that
froths a bit
        but never throws his weight
here's to a statesman
        we should emulate

Of the numerous wonders
        found in nature
snail is by far
        the most privileged creature
chop off his head
        he grows another
quite a stunt
        which should only bother
executioners
        and suchlike thugs
so here's to the envy
        of all mere slugs

You educated owls
     in your gloomy towers
preaching platitudes
     hours and hours
you carcase-sniffers
     you gluttons you fools
you mad-dog bullies
     you cringing mules
time you rallied
     to my call
singing here's to the snail
     an example to us all

A Word to Postumus
after Horace

Remember the shedding calendar
in 40s Hollywood shorthand:
       years tweaked away,
           while you watch and turn grey . . .?

And next thing, it's Big D,
       with the unfunny smile, who
took care of those old-time bigshots
          and *won't* be neglecting you.

    No sooner has Mother Earth
made you feel at home,
than you're off on that one-way, economy cruise,
         never mind what you're worth.

So why should we fret now
      about bombs or crashing planes?
        Why vex our brains
with pollution and global warming?

The same sunless waters
      are on everyone's itinerary;
same grisly entertainments, too.
        Oh yes, you'll see.

    Land, home, adored wife
        must be left behind with life –
all fruits of your labours, except
the timber for your coffin.

    Now picture your swilling heirs
toasting your memory
in vintages you'd laid down
        for your maturer years.

Lullaby for an Orphan
after Pascoli

It snows slow flakes and flakes and flakes
and here is a cradle and here is a child
who sucks his thumb and weeps and wakes
and an old woman sings whose voice is mild

The old woman sings *All round your bed
a garden of lilies and roses is growing
and in that garden your sleepy head*

Slow flakes are snowing are snowing are snowing

Laugh Chant

after Khlebnikov

      Laugh away, laughing boys!
      Laugh along, laughmen!
So they laugh their large laughter, they laugh aloud laughishly.
      Laugh and be laughed at!
O the laughs of the overlaughed, the laughfest of laughingstocks!
      Laugh out uplaughingly the laugh of laughed laughterers!
      Laughily laughterise laughteroids, laughtereens,
           laughpots and laughlings . . .
      Laugh away, laughing boys!
      Laugh along, laughmen!

Little Song

after Baczyński

Who will give me back my rapture
and my shadow, which left when you left?
Days pass like the purring of beasts,
like plants – growing ever younger.

And soon we'll be so small,
we'll find ourselves on board a nutshell,
sailing into the teeth of the seasons
as lightly as if we were skimming whirlpools.

Blood red will appear afresh
in the plump cheeks of the sour cherry.

The iron storm will dwindle back
to the airiness of the dandelion clock.

Tears thundering like a rock-fall
will scatter in the shape of little green beetles.

And, tilting this way and that, we'll sail
without a care towards oblivion,
the only cry for us on earth
coming from our shadows, left behind us.

Catch

after Eliot

Refined and refined
to the same beige-brown sludge
by a baleful mind
which will never be kind
or forget its grudge

the mind of the river
our god and guest
forever departing
unnoticed forever
dispossessed

seeming to doze
from tide to tide
with a slack shrugging
of its broad wrinkled hide
on which a very few craft still ride

but no not slack
not comatose
this brown god lugging
much more in its hurt heart
than on its back

rubbish and wrack
spar and scrap metal
cast aside
broken brittle
and little by little

Edward's Last Stanza

for Ian McEwan

   . . . And so the ferry moves across the bay,
top-heavy as a slice of wedding cake,
leaving us to return to our hotels.
Gulls in nautical trim cry their farewells,
then drop with avaricious eyes to take
souvenirs from the débris of the day.

Some Late-Night Piano
for Charles Simic

As if idly, your man
shuffles and reshuffles
his trusty deck of notes:
their number fixed and few,
their permutations incalculable.

Then he lays out a tune
with its bunches of chords
like a deal in solitaire,
dispassionately, just to give himself
something to work with.

Like a deal in solitaire,
or divination of the future.
Which way will it go?
Will his left hand decide,
or will his right?

They'll settle it between them
in a lilting, lurching
dialogue of the small hours,
sweetly garrulous one minute,
astringent the next.

He, too, is like the king
of a rainy country.
There's a spatter of applause,
but the piano, which knows better,
favours starting afresh.

Lines

for Ian Hamilton

Two blackbirds were pretending to speak Swedish
at four in the morning, as I lay awake
putting the finishing touches to a work
of homage: musical, minimalist, unmodish . . .

No, I wasn't. I was wrenching words
for rhymes – these same, poor, clapped-out hack words –
while out in the garden two never-repetitive blackbirds
were doing their free-jazz thing with the other birds.

North London Sonnet
for Lucinda

A boom-box blats by,
less music than sonic muscle
assaulting the night sky,
a pumped-up hustle-bustle

which manages to disturb
the twirly, needling alarm
of a car tucked into the kerb –
its mantra, or charm –

but that, too, soon quiets
and you sleep on, proof
against the rumpuses and riots
encircling our roof,

till my switching off the light
prompts a muffled *Good night*.

Notes, Acknowledgements and Thanks

Some debts are acknowledged below.

'Palace Floor' appeared in the *Arvon Magazine*.

Michael Hatwell, Christine Fearnside, Jill Hepple and Peter Bostock at Morley College all did rhymed versions of Sebastiano Satta's 'Nella Tanca', helping me with mine.

'To Sylvia' was in *Thumbscrew* No. 19.

Elaine Feinstein invited me to submit some Pushkin translations, of which 'Last Flowers' is one, for her bicentenary anthology, *After Pushkin* (Folio Society, 1999). She supplied a number of English texts for me to work from.

Greek text and crib for Philodemos were in Volume I of *The Greek Anthology*, edited by W. R. Paton (Heinemann, 1916).

At Amherst College, a kind individual whose name I never learned sent me on the trail of Machado's 'Las Moscas'. I could not have followed the Spanish without Alan S. Trueblood's English translation, in his *Antonio Machado: Selected Poems* (Harvard University Press, 1982), alongside. The *London Review of Books* printed 'Flies'.

'A Pipe' and 'Cigar Smoke' appeared together in the *Times Literary Supplement*.

Paul Keegan spotted a howler in my first version of 'Genoa', and gave other advice, improving both this poem and the collection as a whole.

'At the Green Man' and 'Memoirs of a Publisher' were two of three poems grouped under the title 'Eating Out' in *Areté*, Autumn 2000. 'Memoirs of a Publisher' derives from Li Po's 'Self-Abandonment', as rendered by Arthur Waley in his *Chinese Poems* (George Allen & Unwin, 1946).

'Nine Triangles' was written for an exhibition of Breon O'Casey's work at the Oxford Gallery in 1996; was issued later by the artist and Simon King as a lithographic print; and still later appeared, with a sprinkling of typos, in *Breon O'Casey* (The Scolar Press, 1999).

'Thirty-three Paroxysms' was read out on 29 November 2000 at the memorial service for Ewen Henderson (1934–2000), potter, sculptor, painter and friend. Ondt & Gracehoper printed it as a folded sheet for private distribution.

'A Scarecrow's Theory of Art' was for Rob Woolner's show at the Alpha House Gallery, Sherborne, in 1999.

'The Crack' is also the title of a painting by Helen Wilks.

The *TLS* printed 'Espionage', minus its dedication.

'Dogs and Ghosts' was in the final, double issue of *Thumbscrew*, Nos. 20–21.

'Another of Daddy's Cats' was a contribution to *A Parcel of Poems* (Faber and Faber, 1995), celebrating Ted Hughes's sixty-fifth birthday.

Michael Hofmann encouraged me to try my hand at Rilke and I referred both to the German text and to Edward Snow's English in the latter's *New Poems* (1907; North Point Press, 1984).

I came across Elaine Feinstein's translation of 'Sahara' in her *Selected Poems of Marina Tsvetayeva* (Oxford University Press, 1981). Then, pursuing alternative approaches, I found one by Nina Kossman, in her Tsvetayeva selection, *In the Inmost Hour of the Soul* (Humana Press, 1987).

'The Phone-Fox' was in the *Arvon Magazine*.

'Bollockshire' has appeared in the *LRB*.

'Bush to Blair' was written in November 2001.

Translations of 'The Ruin' in *A Choice of Anglo-Saxon Verse* by Richard Hamer (Faber and Faber, 1970) and *The Battle of Maldon and Other Old English Poems* by Kevin Crossley-Holland and Bruce Mitchell (Macmillan, 1965), more faithful than mine, were indispensable.

I owe my discovery of Giuseppe Giusti to Nigel Dennis, who included translations of the Italian poet among poems of his own in *Exotics* (Weidenfeld and Nicolson, 1970); though George Kay's prose trot in *The Penguin Book of Italian Verse* (1958) was a clearer guide in the present exercise.

Gary Kern offers a number of versions of 'Incantation by Laughter', as he titles one of them, in his edition of *Snake Train: Poetry and Prose* by Velimir Khlebnikov (Ardis, 1976).

Natalia Zagórska-Thomas conveyed her enthusiasm for 'Piosenesczka' by Krzysztof Kamil Baczyński (1921–44), showed me her own English version of it and commented on my successive attempts.

Ian McEwan asked me to write the last few lines of a poem with which Edward, a character in his film *The Ploughman's Lunch* (1983), might conclude a poetry reading. Here for the first time I have identified them as 'Edward's Last Stanza'.

'Lines' was commissioned for the festschrift for Ian Hamilton, *Another Round at the Pillars*, edited by David Harsent (Cargo Press, 1999).

I am grateful to all the translators, editors, artists and friends named above, and to those others who have kindly accepted dedications to poems in this book, including my wife, whose position at the fore and aft is conspicuous. I wish it were possible to send as direct a salute to those whose contribution has been less voluntary: the great and the dead whose poems in different languages have attracted or challenged me to make translations or versions of them. While I have received much assistance, I claim all mistakes, distortions and transgressions as my own.